an overbearing eye

an overbearing eye

by
Theodore Michael Christou

First Edition

 Hidden Brook Press
www.HiddenBrookPress.com
writers@HiddenBrookPress.com

an overbearing eye
by Theodore Michael Christou

Front Cover Design – Theodore Michael Christou
Front Cover Photograph – Theodore Michael Christou
Back Cover Photograph – Aglaia Christou
Inside B/W Photographs – Theodore Michael Christou
Layout and Design – Richard M. Grove

Typeset in Arial

Printed and bound in USA

Library and Archives Canada Cataloguing in Publication

Christou, Theodore Michael, 1978-
    An overbearing eye / by Theodore Michael Christou.

(North Shore series ; 26)
Poems.
ISBN 978-1-897475-93-5

    I. Title. II. Series: North Shore series ; 26

PS8605.H7554O94 2012   C811'.6   C2012-906440-8

for my muse
and
for my mother.

Table of Contents

I. i

II. we

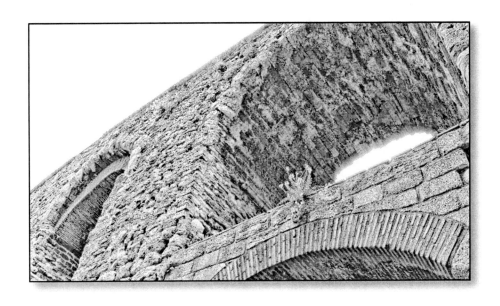

I.
i

contraction

the water was restless as it neared evening. off the southwestern coast of greenland, a fishing trawler veered toward nanortalik. erik gustafson, the captain, held a rectangular mirror speckled with no fewer than seventeen water stains at arms length and gazed intently at his reflection. earlier in the day, when the sun was directly overhead and most overbearing, he had summoned his first mate, lars larsson, to his hold and questioned him about his reasons for permitting the crew of fishermen to sing while they worked. erik despised music and he believed rhyme to be a demon of lyric scale. a ship's crew, he argued, should work as quietly and invisibly as ghosts and as quietly as shadowy whispers. erik spoke to lars animatedly, gesticulating wildly, looking more octopus than man. in fact, lars, who always feared his captain's unpredictable and erratic behaviour, thought for a moment that he was faced with a mythological creature and not a bearded, weathered, angry old man barely five-and-a-half feet tall. the pupils of erik's eyes, out of fear, contracted. erik, noticing this change in the centre of his mate's eyes, was startled and, as a result of the shock, ended the tirade before it had exhausted its full potential.

lars, stoic, left the hold with his head high and went to the deck where his crew awaited instruction. he ordered the pulling in of the nets and the starboard turn of the trawler that pointed its nose home, to nanortalik. the captain, meanwhile, marched to the mirror on the wall above the sink in the neighbouring room. erik looked at himself intently in it, determined to see his own pupils contract. dismayed at the absence of light in the bathroom, he removed the mirror from where it hung from a single rusted and oxidized nail, and took it nearer an oil lamp that rested on a desk in the study across the hall. erik concentrated so intently that he did not hear the men pulling up the nets, the mate shouting instructions, or the writhing of fish suffocating on deck. he did not perceive the change in direction that his trawler took. he did not feel the boat rocking and bobbing on water that had turned reckless.

the sun dipped into the horizon, sizzling as it sank into the water. an airplane, traveling from toronto to london, turned translucent as it moved through the ether above. erik eyed the black holes in the wells of his eyes, and aimed for a miracle of his own.

breathe gently

breathe gently, breeze of fate.
your tempests tire my soul.

as waves upon serene
and silent coasts, constant,
calm, and sure, so sweetly
must you shift and sway each
grain of my spirit's sands.

paleologan

all is made of marble;
i am all, in all, encased. millennia creak and roar, and i lie still.
it was foretold that archangels all aglow with silver and with
gold would descend from the heavens in defense of my life,
but cannons, canons, and ire were proven to be more potent
than prophesy.

all is made of marble. all is ice and glass. all is fable. all is
lost. all is frail mythology. even i am made a myth. in defense
of ancient walls, i fell.

i, ever, howsoever, persevere.

bateau-mouche

i sit by the banks, outcast amidst pairs and lovers.
you see my head, slumped, and pangs of pity swell.
i sneak another glance at my cellular phone, further
avoiding your gaze.

she has yet still yet not called. my face cannot mask
this truth.

i sit by the banks. it is a pretty day and the river
gleams, despite the clouds; despite the threat of rain,
the river-boat passengers wave.

solitary,
standing in cappadocia

i carved my home out of the rock eons ago.
the door still stands, arched. you are welcome
to stand inside with me. therein, within my
home, we shall pray. all is limestone, and
resembles sand sculptures. you may, as i
often have, expect the sea and waves to wash
it all away. my home, and my brothers', and
my sisters' homes, are similarly made of sand
and stone. all are here in cappadocia. here,
as well as to the east.
herein you shall see the blue of our sea, and
red of our blood. the oranges and yellows of
fruit and of fecundity. all is inside the rock,
which we carved, and then elaborated our
faiths upon, eons ago. it has been eons, and
our faces are scratched out. and our tiles are
scraped down. and we remain kneeling,
bearded and cassocked.
we are here, inside the rock. within the pulse
of chants and of music.
lord of red, of blue, and of exquisite colours,
have mercy upon me.

constriction

my pain is a boa, gripping with a
thousand individual scales a
thousand impoverished muscles,
squeezing hips, torso, thighs.

a thousand ohmys have i
whimpered.

but this boa is unmoved by my sighs.

smoke and cold wind

standing in a shivering wind evoked
memories of my birth. the front
steps to my home were fallopian
tubes. the threshold was a
birthday.

yesterday, I wept as a newborn.

today, i stand outside, and i shiver.
the air is cold.
my breath is smoke.

tomorrow i shall pass through to a
different space, via a velvet awning
in the sky. it shall be lovely, and
even my parents would approve.

ambrosia

i long for mother, as all seems lost and futile.
as sleepless nights morph to sleepy days.
as unrest escalates, here and abroad.

i begin to forget those stories,
which she whispered with such dexterity in
the evenings. thetis dipper her son into the river styx,
and mine baptized
me in narrative.

for all affliction, she had song and remedy.

dear mother, hold me.
tell me stories of crafty-minded, or of noble-hearted feats.
put me to sleep with exemplars of courage and of hope.

i long for mother each morning.
her tales are my protection.

my ancestral motherland parts parched and ensanguined lips
and, from her burnished seat
in the cerulean mediterranean,
composes verses of anguish into my extrinsic ears.

with the intrepid determination of the mycenaean fleet, i set
course for the helen of my earth.

there, in the cradle of aphrodite,
where the stony shore accosts the sea and engenders milky,
fragile foam, i found scars left by floods of foreign armies,
a crescent moon scratched upon olympus,
and the furious rage of othello.

i caught a glance of my motherland masked in garish
pageant,
and lit by the counterfeit, ephemeral flash of a camera.

i sought her as she staggered
across the cracks and broken slates,
and athwart stairways that collapsed in the dust of

i blindly sense my passage through streets my parents trod,
and between laborious breaths choked with heat and ash,
i hear the sirens sing stories of a bygone age, forgotten.
i shoulder the burden of historically tragic anamneses,
and blindly theorize upon fanciful meditations
wrought by generations of my oppressed kin.

soon, the scent of the jasmine tickles my senses
and i am locked in the intimate caress of my native soil's
confinement.

the decaying beauty of this land
that justice forgot chokes me with love.

through narrow concourse and parochial pass i pace,
until a wall of extraneous stones,
astounding the very city it divides.

this unfortunately named green line reminds the people
of their plundered land and culture,
and of the peace they do not have.

on this side, an orthodox hymn upsurges to the lord
while, there, the imam's threnody does likewise.
i am not permitted passage.
so i, too, sing:

alluring soil of ardour,
ancient blood swims through your ancient veins.
seek solace, sweet cyprus. let these lyrics balm your pains

green narcissus

the green waters are murky with history. in these, i am
mirrored and blurred.
we have been polluted by time and politicking. by revolution,

and by a too, too long infinity.

which the observed,
and which the doting eyes

there was a bench planted before a painting in the
gallery, upon which i sat to take a brief respite.
this could have been a city park, and the art might
have been a lake, or a wondrous sky.

this was a confrontation with the divine of creation.

the strokes of tinted acrylic were as waves
reflecting stars and light, and so on.

i sat upon this bench, conscious of how my feet
ached. the sandwich in my backpack was
enticing.
the toilets were nearby, i presumed.

the art was gazing at me, as i contemplated
various urges, which wove themselves into the
fabric of my thoughts. this was the christ
pantokrator, whose eyes pursue your gaze
wheresoever you are seated.

the strokes of this master's hand, like the
mysteries of our cosmos, beheld life.
the scene portrayed a stoic face, and the poetics
of this mythic subject rhymed with the words that i
was tacitly composing.

i thought of my sandwich, and i gazed into the
eyes of christ. he, contemplating my many
weaknesses, did not blink.

aurelius, or,
things I say unto myself

i shall not let you surrender here,
though you are rotting.
though you are ripe with age, be wrinkled hope.
though you are turning
soft like slow churned cream, be still like a misty dawn.

you shall fail, and you shall overdo.
you shall, this, too, overcome.

faith subjuncts.

there is goodness.
it shall not be subsumed by any evil, or by any of our
frailties.

breathe fire, and other elements.
breathe, human. storm the angry ramparts.
paint the whole earth blue.

some song to this sea captain there

the banks here
are not as white as dover.
i am not a poet.
this is water, i am man.

the sea-speckled winds spark my cigarettes
and each glows in flickering sequence.

nature and i are akin to little lighthouses.

captain, i can imagine you upon the ship,
distressed by the wind, and distracted by the
flickering sequence of glowing sparks upon the
shore. i presume myself more distressed than you
are,
there upon the sea, although it appears that you
have lost your course. i cannot imagine what you
seek here, where we all are meek. i imagine you
peering imploringly towards the shoals and the
banks. we are frail, flickering, lights.

do not think me a beacon.
i am no symbol, and no sign, despite my little
glowing.

our conversing could not facilitate any navigation
of these swelling waters.
you will surely tire
of listening
to all the gloomy things
that i shall share and say.

do not sink that ship of yours.

do not let me lead you inadvertently unto this
craggled shore.

i am an atom,
small as space,
vast as pinpricks,
lost as faces baked with dirt.

all i know and need is spinning,
i am spinning,
i am spinning,
deriving no salvation from
the bonds with other atom things.

i am atom,
subsitute me for another
like myself and naught is lost.

i, an atom,
quiver in this epic space.

failing to recall a single photograph

the image is somewhat faded. the pond appears grayish,
as opposed to a brilliant blue.
my sideburns are thicker, and my shorts are far too short.

i remember this scene. i remember it otherwise: the
pond, reflecting the fireworks, was byzantine and aflame.
the branches of a willow swept down tenderly and
morosely towards the earth. geese and other lovely
things stretched their necks defiantly, in defense of their
habitat. he wore a white shirt and khaki shorts. she wore
a thin grey sweater with horizontal red stripes and a
flowing skirt.

the image recedes, like unto a distant shore.
memories appear to be mere symbols. my sense of self is
blur and haze.

a white expanse of place and time

i dream of cypress trees and rapids, of the canadian shield, of scarred cliffs of crass waterfalls and of foamy stones.

for a moment, i imagine that i am an explorer. i imagine that in the particular place where i am trespassing, no one has ever stepped.
this is fiction, for someone else has trotted here. there are footprints sunken, still.

this lake is like an artist's pallet.

the snow which covers the waters calls upon me to decorate the blankness and to recreate the white. in the summer, the sun will reflect and shimmer off the waves. now, slumbering beneath the expanse of white, the lake seems subject to my eyes, to my many woes, to my appetites, to my sighs. I shall compose, or paint, upon it.
it remains, despite all my singing, white.

sacrifice of smoke and snow

i wrote my name in
snow, scratching a cigarette
on the bricks of my windowsill.
perhaps all who have
sat on beaches have done likewise with their fingers, in the sand.

my action lacked originality.

the wind, shifting powder and snow, erased my name away.

i wrote my name again in letters more prominent

the filter scuffed against the
brick, and the smell of the wafting smoke in the cold air drifted
slowly unto the heavens appeasing my gods.

my intention is not permanence
or reflection, but sacrifice.

life, like letters in the snow and sand, is a reminder of
impermanence.

fear eating

fear is a delicious word.
it is not bad. it is not all bad.

fear of god is, for instance, in various contexts, virtuous.
quivering kierkegards and kafkas have yoked fear to trembling
and, more importantly, to courage.

to be fearful is often to be far from bombast.

fear is delicious, contested,
heavy. like most ideas worthy of debate fear is a friend to verse.

love, on the contrary, the subject of so much poetry, remains so
elusive to poets.
love cannot be subject to debate. love cannot be contested.
love is.

love is, and it cannot, as a consequence, be made. making, on
the contrary, is the business of poetry.

i can, therefore, say nothing of love.

stepping into a river, twice

all shall change to fire, according to primordial nature.
thereafter, exhausted, as heraclitus had predicted,
all shall be restored, renewed.

as moisture in the air drips
downwards
on the glass of windowpanes,
slipping tearfully,
following a change of matter:
       so shall all change to flame
       so shall all burn to ash
       so shall all change again to flame,
       according to nature and to presocratic thought.
we step here into flood and rushing waters;
slipping, the whole world flows by
and by. it all looks so familiar:
       all the horror, the flame, the ash.

yet each quake, each flood, each fire is unique; we cannot
step into the same river, twice.
all dissolves, and all is renewed; qualitatively inimitable.

epictetus

daylight is leaking through the blinds. this is a zebra morning.
leaves are turning phosphorescent red. branches bearing both red and green foliage, which my window frames, wave in the wind. the trunk of the maple stands firm and constant.

rain falls consistently. it is in no hurry. the humidity has broken. the air conveys the sense that some tyrant has been overthrown. i breathe more easily.

wind waves through the yard and into the room, ushering about a new age.

the news reports that, elsewhere, a hurricane rages. ships are being diverted, homes are being uprooted, shores are flooding, and panic prevails.

this, and that, shall pass.
there, and here, we persevere.

fairer form

leaves fade from green,
as fathers' hairs from fair hues fail with age, i thought.
leaves fall from grace, as failing lives
cede strength and breath,
in death, i thought.

leaves fall for thee,
sweet faith, i see, to grace thy steps, which grace the
streets.

green youth leaves all, who in love fall;
in fairer form,
we are reborn.

on archetypes

an empty can rumbled by on the sidewalk, caving in and
crumbling as it tumbled. rumbling by, unburdened, it
hastened to keep pace with the winter wind.
i thought to assuage it.

this bumbling can evoked in me great sympathy. i was
reminded of times when i felt as spent and as disavowed as
a vacant vessel tossed about.

i turned, and went indoors.
out of the wind, i sat by my window and waited for another
metaphor—fumbling, perhaps—to blow by, before me.

crimson

in one moment
  .i seized the monument
  .it was passion

  .anger.

i threw it up into the scarlet sky

  .to hell with marble and grace.

II.
we

the underweaving we

this is a love story. a mystery, also. this love story is not wholly imagined. i mention this observation on imagination not in passing, nor in careless skimming of aims at verisimilitude, but because i've recently read that history does not replicate mythology. this thought threatens to extrapolate itself here into a manifesto and, with uncharacteristic self-restraint of tongue, i will only gloss off its relevance to the second sentence typed. assume, then, that this is a mythology you read, it follows that the plot will not play out in the forum of history that you witness, for example, on the evening news. i dispute this virulently, however, and force completion to this thought by saying that there is not myth that is not planted in the mirror of memory and life.

this story, then, commences in a frame. danielle is twenty four years old and she sits, legs outstretched, on a bed in her dormitory. her back leans on a pillow pushed against the grey wall and her head arches forward, bent by concentrated reading. the concrete walls are a testament to cold, thus necessitating the pillow.

the classic description, as a professor of french canadian literature once mentioned in a lecture, begins with the top of the head and, with clinically literal precision, ends with the tip of the toes. i'm paraphrasing her who, to the best of my memory, was more a pretty face than a learned scholar. she may have been correct in this, but i am no flaubert and danielle is no madame bovary. besides, flaubert was not french canadian and his celebrated novel bored me to cynicism.

this is the point in the story where i stop writing unnaturally.

please forget her name and place.

her eyes are as round and as wet as wading pools. the children splashing and dancing in knee-high waters are not only images in your memory conjured by image because i see them in her open eyes.

she listens to the drumbeat in the background of the song on the radio as she reads. her mind's foreground is either on the novel in her hands or on the thumping in her ears. probably the latter. her head bobs to the beat.

she puts down the book. folding the corners of pages is a brutal way of bookmarking that she only practices on texts loaned from the public library. don't judge, these books are most likely folded anyway (in the most peculiar places and not, for example, always at the end of a chapter or narrative stream). regardless, there's an old picture of her cousin that she fits between the pages she's been reading before sitting her book on the floor beside her bed.

she sits up straighter than before and writes this poem:

morning of my echoes
bear the trespass of unfurling hymns
i am air
and this   my sickness
wanes
as silver's self-reflections wear
as waters wane
as even tempests tire
as the moon sleeps to defy the sun
this is the one
the morning of my echoes

she writes in a hardcover journal with a brown false leather cover. The texture of it is not of poor enough quality to have adverse affects on her verse. a recurrent suspicion that lingers in her mind, though, is that if she were writing with a mont blanc fountain pen on thick parchment or on an antique scroll, her writing would be of a higher constitution.

she writes irregularly and regularly. it depends on the weather.

once she had a dream that her hair, which curls in blond and auburn tresses to her shoulders, was crowned with a wreath of small white flowers. she spun, twirled rather, in beams of streaking sunlight that broke through foliage of tall rich trees on the brink of an enchanted wood. a stream, i think she remembers, fluttered out of sight over a hill farther than her eyes could see. the grass was lush, untrimmed, and of the most emerald hue of green. only the butterflies, rising and falling in a ritual flight, where absent, though as she spun she scanned for them.

and even as turns are quantifiable, in respect to speed or number of rotations, for example, there was nought to be measured in this dream (with the notable exception of the absence of butterflies, however) besides her bliss. Each spin recalled the majesty of a cyclone and each turn was true epic, long and slow.

she did not dream him.

he wore his obscurity in the same manner he would model a white fur coat – uncomfortably. he looks, with wide-eyed wonder, at the haze of sparkling star-specks in the black night sky until the scene swirls and his insides curl with grief.

the ignominy of his self-concept does not derive from a desire to be celebrated and revered. dim moonlight is more pleasant than the neon name of fame.

no one hears themselves whispering in the faltering music of his songs. he needs someone to weep, hearing his songs, as he does in their composition. understanding. it is as if he flutters in a vacuum, in a void. out of sight of one who might, in feeling, hear.

it is midnight, at least. he walks, oblivious to all but the evanescent shimmer of his mistress, and he sings, beneath his breath, to her:

maid;
my mistress
moon
;i am uncovered
winter's white is here
;it holds me
in a frozen gaze;
in this stuttered phrase
of song
;my mistress;
make of me
a butterfly;
i crawl this night so low;

and dream me
in the snowfall's shade;
below the breaking change of days;
near sorrow's lazy
forest glades;
to fly in my imperfect ways;
where angels spinning sin
;desiring;
sing
in moonshine rhythms
;mistress
;pray
;i want my wings.

the song went on, inconclusively, for a period, before turning back on itself and re-using several of the most interesting rhymes and images, transmuting them to uselessness.

he never dreamt her, through he sang of her and through the moon's reflecting vigour, invited her to him.

this is love.

her eden lacked, of him. his lyric locked, on her.

they never meet, i think. they should, but matters of love and loss are the greatest mysteries. in such matters, investigations are of great redundancy.

this is love. they are not wrought of self-need. neither is meaning lost in touch or by touching. one's desire is not fuelled by ambition for the other.

their love is perfect. it preserves the mystery.

and this will have to suffice.

fisher boy

and if all life, then, were a sea,
a drunken world into itself

with mountain ridges, peaks, and cliffs,
or chasms, trenches, gutters, troughs, and cracks,
dirt, rock, mineral, and loam,
movement, breath,
fight, toil, and sport,

i would be a shoeless fisher boy,
and our love would be a shrimp,
beady-headed shelled and hard,
like a cockroach of the sea,
armed in pink, a fairy knight,
with eyes ugly as a whip.

it drags and crunches in the mud,
with ugly legs too small and weak
to more than scuttle,
too encumbered by its carcass
and its dense and gross imbalance
to swim.

i the fisher,
taste its sweet and meaty
flesh. i love the crack
upon its tail,
and all the biting.

ugly love,
you are the glory
of all life under the sea.

to my taste,
you are enchanting.

i fish only now
for thee.

we have profound
thanks to offer

upon waking, tremor shook me
it was early in the morning. it was late into the night.
our house was still and quiet. all was silent as a candle.
my heart paced, all aflame, and darker than yellow.
our bedroom had all the feeling of a tabernacle.
i woke, quaking. waking, i saw you beside me. silent, as a
candle. bright, alight, a flame.

you shifted slightly, as I wrapped myself around your
shoulder. you shielded me from the quiet night.

someday, i shall do the same.

persephone

into the grey of our quiet morning climbed a vine
of life's distress. drudgery rises as anxiety within
and in between us, nurtured by the rain outside.
it climbs neither as slowly as grape vines grow,
nor does it race, like racy lingerie.

toil is patient as a hospital ward. it is persistent
as rain.
i could have slept a day today, and you might
have slept for weeks. i saw it in your green-
turned-hazel gaze, which turned towards me in
the hallway, that you've been contemplating the
benefits of hibernation for human happiness.

my love, you are that very same sunshine that the
sunshine mocks. spread that light throughout the
world this morning. beam, despite the toil of work.

it has rained relentlessly.
your labours are as vital as nature's are. with
regards to brightness, you are persephone.

only, you hair is infinitely more lovely.

a vegetable ball, of toast and feasts and time

there is time for toast and feasting in the
morning. haste is waste of breath and life.
we do naught but tend to toil and suffering,
whilst our beauties age and grey.

you are lovely. beauty, rise and make the
mornings blush.

the pace of life is torrid, as a current it
sweeps us along.

there is more time to gaze. to toast and feast and
laugh. to crawl out of the current,
and to bask upon the sandy banks. to
sleep and laugh, and love.

demonstration d'amour propre

on a ribald morning, we sat at our kitchen table. it was
seasonably cold, but unseasonably sad outside. you asked
me to wear a paisley tie.
the colour of the tie was regal. you had purchased it years
ago, and it had only recently resurfaced, garnering several
comments and notes of praise at work, where i wore it.
further, this tie matched in hue(more than in colour)your very
pretty porphyry dress.
we sat there(me: initially, obligingly, but, ultimately,
begrudgingly. you: you grinned like a ginger cat) at our little
kitchen table, drinking tea. you wore your pretty dress, and i,
my paisley tie.
there were many chores to do, despite the cold, despite the
sad, despite the tie and tea. we were of a certain age. our
hair was teasing us with silver inflection. our bellies had
begun to droop. we found morning hints of paisley and
porphyry playful.
o, dear, how i loved you. i must overturn my clothes and
closet to find my lost paisley tie.

if it were yesterday

by the long banks of this broad
and murky water
was a fair and tender reed.
it was solitary
and it filled me with longing.

that was earlier today.

if it were yesterday,
where the bright sun pierced my
melancholy
and the air echoed light,
it might have been otherwise.

we, in impression and in act,
have been otherwise.
less solitary.
less like lonely reeds.

life and earth, as cedar

we have heard it said that the earth,
and its demise, are, alternatively: fire,
wind, ice, and water. there are, i would imagine,
other catastrophes
prophesied to destroy the world,
and other sources of our existence.

i would posit that all of these amount to love,
or, that all of these are
reducible to love.

we have, likewise, perhaps almost entirely,
heard of love in terms of
consuming heat. i have seen love, as a fire,
burn and devour. plans and
constitutions ignite and turn to ash. love is primordial.

all else is kindling.

we conversed once following a reading. it was following
my second reading. i am alone at readings,
embarrassed when i choke
and cry at awkward moments.
　　but i met you, and we conversed.
i enjoyed your poem, you exclaimed.
slow down when you read, so the words do not all blur together.
also, there is no need to cry.

　　　　　　later, that evening,
during a dinner party, i made the peculiar decision to ask
of a friend's wife if she would write for me a poem.

me, a poem. i don't know
how, she retorted, flustered.
I exclaimed something to the effect of:
you cannot know if you can or cannot, unless you try.

　　i exclaimed the above but i was thinking about something
　　we said during our conversation, which concerned the
purposes of poetry.
　　i was thinking: anyone
　　　　can write a poem, lady. just
　　demonstrate a little creativity in form,
　　and don't let the lines you write always reach
　　the end of the page. you can do that and still be writing
　　poetry. poetry is not just form.

this thinking was altogether quite confusing,
particularly if you situate it in the context
of an awkward conversation at a dinner party.
conversations with great poets throw my words off kilter.
    the kind lady replied to my entreaty and off kilter explanations;
    but

        i did not
        hear her words because
        i was caught up in my
        internal dialogue.

all of creation is an epic poem, i concluded to myself.
we, all, are verse. this,
here,
is a miniature universe, which i have scripted in your honour.

aftershock (or, cowering in a corner)

the force of your desires is seismic. it is all tumbled and
quivered as a consequence. it shivers and quakes. i hear a
truck rolling outside the window, and i think it the
apocalypse. conversely, a chirping bird hearkens unto
angelic hosts, and the world turns weightless or
ascendent(depending upon the time of day).

a shiver, and i expect the pyramids to fall. a smirk, and
concrete of my constitution ripples, cracking into fractal
patterns.

a pitter and a patter of laughter, and the cosmos ceases
to shake.

tu me bouleverse.

i am entirely subject to your whims.

through you, in me

i turned away from love purposefully.

i turned towards all that seemed to be
ugly like me. in idea and in image.

yet beauty was there, everywhere.
even in its apparent absence. in there.
in all, was beauty.
in all, in you.

through you, in me.

withdrawing to a restless space

it is dark.
i am surprised by the rain, which
competes with the ticking clock on my
bed stand for my attention.
both are desperate for my attention.

the sensation of heaviness pervades
both head and soul;

you sleep, my beauty. it is a delight to
watch you breathe. but i shan't linger.
lingering is creepiness.

i retreat for another night to the second
bed. by god, darling, rest.
your eyes have been tired. mine are
restless.

the rain repeats it's lonely drumming
upon our window pane. it's ticking
seems apace with the clicking clock
beside my lonely bed.

holy grace

i long for grace. i pursue her
shadows

through the cracks and black, through
love and lace. via hope, through lost
belongings.

i baptize her; i take her on travails
and to sleezy motels. i gawk with her
at neon, and i weep, transcribing
lyrics that are tender as stones.

i long, but grace
remains my hope, my might, a
whispering divination, air,

all mercy and atonement.

some thing akin to a machete

there were occasions when i spied you from afar,
walking, swaying hips, flipping tresses.

once, immoderate and unrestrained by your
movements, i found a purveyor of already-twisted
balloon animals. i purchased his stock in its entirety
and lay it before your path as if it were a silicon zoo.

you are, as always, evocative. your movements still
evoke in my childhood fictions. i lose my adulthood
when you smile.

you were once walking in the wind, by a fountain, in a
beautiful city during the spring. this walking was all art.

i see you walking now, and i notice neither swaying nor flipping. the art is like the mayan temple overcome by time and by the natural growth of jungles. you are temple, and my worries are the jungle.

fetch some thing akin to a machete, dear. i'm hell bent on treasure hunting.

the air was all cliché and elemental.

we could have thrown seeds into the
air as we drove past fields and plots
of houses with the windows open,
and these seeds would have
flowered.
there suspended in the air, roots
might have sprouted.

it was as if the earth was thick with
matter and with antiquity.

herbs and flora were spirit. their aura
was suspended in the density.
our thoughts, too, took root in the
landscape.

we breathed it in, all the cliché and
element.
and, breathing, we felt well fed.

once upon an afternoon
in a sunny space

our movements in the car were
liberating.

we were restrained by belts,
fastenedtightly. cordoned off by
vinyl and by metal buckles from the
swoosh of air, from the sun.
but the movements liberated us;
within restrained space. the
          music shook us from our
stillness.

the music was dated. the steel
design of our frame was dated.
dated was the technology, the hair,
the clothes, and
theturnsthetwists of phrase.

but our movements in the car were
ancient, and they were profound in
their humanity.

wistful, otherwise

bring me to that hill we passed whilst on the
train to the palace.

you tapped my thigh, interrupting nothing.
you nodded. you gestured so that my sight
might pursue the direction of our gaze. i
pursued, gazing in tune.
each inch of the dwarfish mount we
looked
upon was populated. it was all built upon,
passing quickly beyond our sight. i
imagined each home as a vibrant space.

it was a happy space, i now recall.
on that rapid july afternoon, flooded by light
and heat, i contemplated living otherwise.
life could be otherwise.

take me there, to the mount. take me to
july, and all shall be well. I shall
perchance,
there, sleep.

feasting, baking in the sun

the island was dust. the summers were
particularly arid. the sun wrinkled our eyes. its
heat baked our lungs, which were full of dust
and sand.
grandfather was a shepherd. we rode out on a
tractor to tend to the flock; he drove, and i gripped
to the backward-facing wooden board on which i
sat.

grandfather and I would sit out in the sun baking.
from a satchel he would draw out a large loaf that
grandmother had baked in the clay domed
woodstove(onto which i made a mark each
morning with a sharp stone stashed by the wire
fence. grandfather's knife was sharp as wit.
grandfather would carve a perfect slice of bread,
then another.

wrapped in a cloth were green olives grandmother had
picked and pickled, dressed with crushed coriander and
with olive oil.

a slightly larger was enshrouded a hard piece of halloumi.
i had been inexpertly milking goats here over the summer,
hunched over a pail made of some metal. this was last
year's cheese, which we were preparing to eat, salty and
flavoured with dry mint.

we sat baking in the sun in a land baked by
millennia of war and occupation.

amidst the dust, beneath the sun, we feasted. we
ate the fruits of this island place and became part
of the earth, dust, and sand.

sometime, walking home

i was in the epicenter,
where winds converged.

lights, elongated like shadows, waved,
emanating from both sides of the river,
seemingly concerned with the locus of their reflection.

we were not retiring,
despite the knowledge that the night was alert,
and that the winds, waters, and lights observed us.

we were leaning on the edge of an epicenter(an epicenter
that we had decided upon, and contrived), breathing warmth
into the chill air.

pausing, in retreat of myth

oh, but there is so much to see, to spend, to taste.

alas for our red-dry eyes. alas for the cost and regrets. alas that we both shall die.

oh, but today, i do not hear the fearful rumble of chariot steel pursuing.

hades, too, has much to do.

and we must indulge our senses.

supplicant as a fresco

you are my regent.

i offer you a gift of grain
and wine.

these are the offspring of my labours,
which are all for you
to honour, as i love.

my skin is baked and crusted,
smelling of sun and sweat
it stretches taught, like leather,
tanned.

bent
beneath your gaze,
i visualize how my modest torso is perceived,
and whether it is revolting.
Surely, it does not entice.

kneeling, with more strain,
curling my spine to touch chin to knee,
bending my face into a grimace
at an angle that shadows me from your grace,
i supplicate.
i suspect you are revolted,
and that my modest gift does not entice.
you neither smile, nor do you grimace.

seconds are as minutes,
while eons evolve and change the contexts and continents,
which are mutable, unlike our constant pose.
stars are born and spent before us.
bonfires spin,
and rocks repose.

but, still, we stay.
but, still, you stay above me.

this night

this night, I write
for you, and because of you.

because I cannot sleep. because I cannot stretch
my grin and pleasure
farther athwart my face. because I look silly.
because of my silly smile.
because I endeavoured to hurdle over a fence, and fell.

and i laughed all the louder.

because you are not here, despite dominating my thoughts.
because I cannot sleep,
seemingly unwilling to let go of this day, which
brims with thoughts of you.

because the impulse grips me.
and because my pulse is pacing.
and because my whims are racing
me ever towards you.

because i'm fearful of this feeling,
which is like a love-know that tethers
me
tightly.

and because
        i
        feel
        i'm
        falling.

and because
i've fallen, quite.

contrition

i loved you ere i saw you.
i dreamt you ere i slept.
i prayed for you and crafted you
with wisps of fancy and fright.

each night, your spirit sang to me,
each night, in wait, i wept.
each night i pledged my love for you –
ere i knew you; ere i saw you; ere we met.

Books in the North Shore Series

Find full information at
– http://www.HiddenBrookPress.com/b-NShore.html

Anthologies

Changing Ways is a book of prose by Cobourg area authors including: Jean Edgar Benitz, Patricia Calder, Fran O'Hara Campbell, Leonard D'Agostino, Shane Joseph, Brian Mullally. Editor: Jacob Hogeterp – Prose – ISBN – 978-1-897475-22-5

That Not Forgotten - Editor – Bruce Kauffman with 118 authors – Prose and Poetry – ISBN – 978-1-897475-89-8

First set of five books

— **M.E. Csamer** – Kingston – *A Month Without Snow* – Prose – ISBN – 978-1-897475-87-2
— **Elizabeth Greene** – Kingston – *The Iron Shoes* – Poetry – ISBN – 978-1-897475-76-6
— **Richard Grove** – Brighton – *A Family Reunion* – Prose – ISBN – 978-1-897475-90-2
— **R.D. Roy** – Trenton – *A Pre emptive Kindness* – Prose – ISBN – 978-1-897475-80-3
— **Eric Winter** – Cobourg – *The Man In The Hat* – Poetry – ISBN – 978-1-897475-77-3

Second set of five books

— **Janet Richards** – Belleville – *Glass Skin* – Poetry – ISBN – 978-1-897475-01-0
— **R.D. Roy** – Trenton – *Three Cities* – Poetry – ISBN – 978-1-897475-96-4
— **Wayne Schlepp** – Cobourg – *The Darker Edges of the Sky* – Poetry – ISBN – 978-1-897475-99-5
— **Benjamin Sheedy** – Kingston – *A Centre in Which They Breed* – Poetry – ISBN – 978-1-897475-98-8
— **Patricia Stone** – Peterborough – *All Things Considered* – Prose – ISBN – 978-1-897475-04-1

Third set of five books

— **Mark Clement** – Cobourg – *Island In the Shadow*
  – Poetry – ISBN – 978-1-897475-08-9
— **Anthony Donnelly** – Brighton – *Fishbowl Fridays*
  – Prose – ISBN – 978-1-897475-02-7
— **Chris Faiers** – Marmora – *ZenRiver Poems & Haibun*
  – Poetry – ISBN – 978-1-897475-25-6
— **Shane Joseph** – Cobourg – *Fringe Dwellers* Second Edition
  – Prose – ISBN – 978-1-897475-44-7
— **Deborah Panko** – Cobourg – *Somewhat Elsewhere*
  – Poetry – ISBN – 978-1-897475-13-3

Forth set of five books

— **Diane Dawber** – Bath – *Driving, Braking and Getting out to Walk*
  – Poetry – ISBN – 978-1-897475-40-9
— **Patrick Gray** – Port Hope – *This Grace of Light*
  – Poetry – ISBN – 978-1-897475-34-8
— **John Pigeau** – Kingston – *The Nothing Waltz*
  – Prose – ISBN – 978-1-897475-37-9
— **Mike Johnston** – Cobourg – *Reflections Around the Sun*
  – Poetry – ISBN – 978-1-897475-38-6
— **Kathryn MacDonald** – Shannonville – *Calla & Édourd*
  – Prose – ISBN – 978-1-897475-39-3

Fifth set of three books

— **Tara Kainer** – Kingston – *When I Think On Your Lives*
  – Poetry– ISBN – 978-1-897475-68-3
— **Morgan Wade** – Kingston – *The Last Stoic*
  – Novel – ISBN – 978-1-897475-63-8
— **Kathryn MacDonald** – Shannonville – *A Breeze You Whisper*
  – Poetry – ISBN – 978-1-897475-66-9

Sixth set of three books

—**Bruce Kauffman** – *The Texture of Days, in Ash and Leaf*
  – Poetry – ISBN - 978-1-897475-86-7
— **Chris Faiers** – *Eel Pie Island Dharma: A hippie memoir/haibun*
  – A memoir in haibun form – ISBN - 978-1-897475-92-8
— **Theodore Michael Christou** – *an overbearing eye*
  – Poety – ISBN – 978-1-897475-93-5